THE TREACHERY
OF IMAGES

ANDREW BISS

Copyright © Andrew Biss 2017

CAUTION: Professionals and amateurs are hereby warned that *The Treachery of Images* is subject to a royalty. It is fully protected under the copyright laws of the United States of America, the British Commonwealth, including Canada, and all other countries of the Copyright Union. All rights, including professional, amateur, motion picture, recitation, lecturing, public reading, radio broadcasting, television, and the rights of translation into foreign language are strictly reserved.

Royalty of the required amount must be paid whether the play is presented for charity or gain and whether or not admission is charged. All performance rights, licensing and royalty arrangements are to be made through the following direct contact address: info@andrewbiss.com

Copying from this book in whole or in part is strictly forbidden, and the right of performance is not transferable.

Due authorship credit must be given on all programs, printing and advertising for the play.

No one shall make changes in this play for the purpose of production without written permission. Publication of this play does not imply availability for performance.

No part of this book may be reproduced, stored in a retrieval system, or transmitted in any form, by any means, including mechanical, electronic, photocopying, recording, videotaping or otherwise, without prior written permission of the author.

Original cover image © stocksnapper

Cover design by Ernest Waggenheim

First Printing, 2017

All rights reserved.

ISBN-13: 978-1546518426
ISBN-10: 1546518428

ENTR'ACTE
EDITIONS

"Everyone says forgiveness is a lovely idea, until they have something to forgive."

C. S. Lewis.

THE TREACHERY OF IMAGES

The world premiere of *The Treachery of Images* was presented in a staged reading by Heiress Productions at Simple Studios in New York in 2011.

The play was directed by Marisa Viola with the following cast:

Christine Wilkes...................................Amanda Ladd
Tom Wilkes...Randy Noojin

CHARACTERS

CHRISTINE WILKES: Riven with grief and anger. Trenchant, hard exterior masks a need to connect. 40s/50s.

TOM WILKES: Restrained and level-headed, but not unflappable. Rational, sometimes to the point of appearing impassive. 40s/50s.

SETTING & TIME

SETTING: The living room of the Wilkes' home in a London suburb.

TIME: The present.

PLAYWRIGHT'S NOTE

I have endeavoured to keep the inclusion of stage directions to a minimum in this script, noting only those considered necessary, as I do not believe they can be established in a play such as this until the rehearsal process begins. I have, however, placed greater emphasis on the application of silence, the orchestration of which is a fundamental element of the play's shape and character.

The Treachery of Images

At Rise: The lights come up on an empty living room. The room itself is well-kept and comfortably furnished in an unremarkable middle-class style. There is a sofa, armchairs, end tables, etc., and a sideboard upstage C., which also serves as a bar. On the centre of the sideboard is a framed photograph of a young woman. Presently, the sound of someone descending a staircase is heard. Soon after, CHRISTINE slowly enters, carrying a medium-sized suitcase. She places the suitcase in the middle of the room and stares at it for some time. At last overcome with emotion, she drops to the floor, clutching the suitcase to her body and attempting to stifle her cries. Moments later the sound of someone entering through the front door is heard.

TOM: (*Off.*) Hello? (*Beat.*) Hello? (*Beat.*) Anyone home?

> (*CHRISTINE immediately attempts to regain her composure. She seats herself on the sofa, placing the suitcase by her side, and wipes her eyes with her hands. Moments later, TOM enters the room. CHRISTINE remains motionless.*)

TOM: Oh, you are here. Didn't you hear me?

> (*TOM fixes himself a scotch from the bar on the sideboard.*)

TOM: Don't know why I said "anyone" come to think of it, since it could only be you.

> (*Beat.*)

CHRISTINE: Quite.

> (*Beat.*)

TOM: Yes, well it's um…just one of those things one says, I suppose.

(TOM *picks up his glass and begins to cross to CHRISTINE.*)

TOM: Funny how these habits sort of–

(TOM *suddenly he notices the suitcase. He stops in his tracks. Pause.*)

TOM: What's that?

(*Beat.*)

CHRISTINE: That? (*Beat.*) That is exactly what it looks like, Tom. It is a suitcase. Ceci est un valise.

TOM: Thank you for clarifying. And may I ask what it's doing there?

(*Beat.*)

CHRISTINE: Coming with me.

TOM: I rather gathered that. I meant…why?

CHRISTINE: Isn't it obvious?

TOM: Not necessarily. Why don't you try me?

CHRISTINE: What a waste of breath that would be.

TOM: Not if it changed your mind.

CHRISTINE: Let's not, shall we?

TOM: Why not?

CHRISTINE: Because there's nothing to say.

TOM: Well, if you didn't want to talk then why didn't you just go?

CHRISTINE: Because…

TOM: Why sit here waiting for me?

   (*Beat.*)

CHRISTINE: Because I'm not the kind of person who runs from their responsibilities, that's why.

TOM: No…just me, apparently.

CHRISTINE: I face things.

TOM: So if you're not running just yet, then let's talk.

   (*Pause.*)

CHRISTINE: And what is it you want to talk about, exactly? The weather? The rising sea levels? The war in Afghanistan? *Your day?*

TOM: Us, of course.

CHRISTINE: And what on earth would we gain in doing that?

TOM: Well, for starters…how about some understanding.

CHRISTINE: How about we don't.

(*Beat.*)

TOM: Try…for me?

CHRISTINE: Best not to pick at scabs, don't you think? (*Beat.*) Besides…I haven't the will.

TOM: Yes…that's more to the point, isn't it? That's what's at the root of all this. You've let it beat you. You've admitted defeat.

CHRISTINE: Oh, what the hell do you expect?

TOM: Expect? I expect you to fight, that's what I expect. I don't expect you to just roll over and play dead.

CHRISTINE: For Christ's sake, Tom, don't you understand, I already *am* dead!

TOM: Oh, stop being so ridiculous! And stop talking like that. Honestly, I can't…I don't understand you. It's as if you've…cloaked yourself in defeatism. It's like a…a shroud you've wrapped yourself in. (*Beat.*) And if you're so bloody good at facing up to things, then it's about time you acknowledged that you've got the rest of your life ahead of you and you can't go through it playing the perpetual bloody victim all the time.

(*Pause.*)

CHRISTINE: Can't I? So what would you say I am, then?

TOM: What?

CHRISTINE: What am I, if not a victim?

TOM: You're someone who has a choice. A choice between giving in to the vagaries of life or fighting back and trying to make something of it.

CHRISTINE: "The vagaries of life"? Is that what you're calling it now?

TOM: I didn't mean it like—

CHRISTINE: My God, it didn't take you long to trivialize it down to something bite-size and chewable, did it?

TOM: All I meant was—

CHRISTINE: Oh, I know exactly what you meant. But I'm sorry, I'm afraid I can't hide the ugly truth behind pat phrases and quaint adages. Good God, next you'll be telling me "When life hands you lemons…"

TOM: Now you're being flippant.

CHRISTINE: *Me?*

TOM: Yes. You know damn well what I was saying. And since you bring it up, I'm not asking you to make lemonade, I'm asking you to stop chewing on them.

CHRISTINE: Oh, very clever. Very…pithy.

TOM: Very bitter.

CHRISTINE: Yes…that's right, I am bitter, Tom. I'm very bitter.

And I make apologies for it. Why would I when I have every reason in the world for feeling bitter?

    (Beat.)

TOM: You don't have to be.

CHRISTINE: I know I don't *have* to be. No one's born bitter. It's something acquired over time. It's one of the benefits of experience.

    (Beat.)

TOM: Look, all I'm asking you to…you just need to pull yourself up out of this. To make something of what's left.

CHRISTINE: And what might that be? What exactly do we have left now?

    (Beat.)

TOM: Us.

CHRISTINE: Ah…that word again. *(Beat.)* The problem is…there's a you and a there's a me, but I don't believe that there is an "us" anymore.

TOM: Of course there is. There is if you want there to be…if you're willing to fight for it.

CHRISTINE: Goodness, all of this fighting. Where do you get the energy?

TOM: Figure of speech.

CHRISTINE: Yes, well…figuratively speaking, I've hung up my gloves. The fight's over.

TOM: It's not, I'm afraid. It's just beginning.

CHRISTINE: It is for me.

TOM: But…that's because you can't get out of your own way long enough to even think straight. You've let this…it's locked you down…it's like you're…you're paralyzed. How can you possibly know how you feel about us – about me – when you won't even allow yourself to feel?

CHRISTINE: I sometimes wonder if there ever was an "us."

TOM: Oh, for God's sake!

CHRISTINE: In the beginning, I suppose. But looking back…

TOM: Always looking back.

CHRISTINE: What was it? (*Beat.*) What was it really?

    (*Pause.*)

TOM: I thought it was love.

CHRISTINE: Yes, exactly. I'm sure I did, too.

TOM: It was for me.

CHRISTINE: But I wonder now if it was really just…a close approximation?

TOM: A what?

CHRISTINE: Because it's all so new, isn't it, when you're young? So how are you supposed to know?

TOM: You don't know it, you feel it.

CHRISTINE: Yes, but how do you know what you're you feeling? How do you know if it's the real thing or…or just something close to it? How do you know the difference? I mean, you're young and everything's new, and…then one day you meet someone and you find yourselves attracted to each other, and you share things in common and you make each other laugh and feel special and important in ways you'd never felt before, and it's all rather like being a little drunk. And while it's all still heady and intoxicating, you find yourselves making all kinds of plans and commitments for the future, and you're so caught up in it all that you don't even notice the buzz wearing off. It all becomes a blur of years and events, of birthdays and anniversaries, highs and lows…a lifetime. And you never stop to re-examine it…not really. Because it's done. And you're scared to. So you don't. (*Beat.*) Not until something…

    (*Pause.*)

TOM: So…this was all a great mistake, was it?

CHRISTINE: I'm…I'm not saying that.

TOM: Sure as hell sounded like it.

CHRISTINE: No, it's not…I'm not…that's not what I meant.

TOM: Then what?

CHRISTINE: Just that...perhaps that's how it is for everyone. Perhaps that's all it is. We all get drunk on emotion and stagger down some path together thinking we've found love, when all along it was just...a close approximation.

    (Beat.)

TOM: Even if you were right – and I'm not saying you are – but even if that is all it is...then surely that's the best you can hope for, isn't it – to get that close?

CHRISTINE: Yes...I suppose it is. *(Beat.)* Back to your lemons.

TOM: For Christ's sake, Christine, you're talking like some lovelorn bloody teenager. Of course the sparks don't last. They never do – not for anything. It's what's left behind, that's important. Two people building a life together, making something meaningful out of it all.

    (Beat.)

CHRISTINE: Two.

    (Beat.)

TOM: Now.

    (Beat.)

CHRISTINE: Yes.

    (Pause.)

TOM: I can't bring her back, Christine.

CHRISTINE: Oh stop it, will you? Stop it with these stupid bloody platitudes! Stop trying to sound like you're the one who's being rational and realistic when we both know nothing could be further from the truth.

TOM: Of course I am.

CHRISTINE: You're not! You are not! You know damn well you're not!

TOM: (*Calmly.*) Christine, I am dealing with this in the only healthy way that a person can.

CHRISTINE: (*Incredulous.*) Healthy? *Healthy?* What in God's name is *healthy* about any of this? There is no *cure* for this. It's all a fucking cancer!

    (*Pause.*)

TOM: Susan's life is over. Ours are not. The only *healthy* way for us to move forward from this is to accept what has happened, to forgive what has happened, and to move on.

CHRISTINE: Ah, yes…and *there* it is. There's that great, lumbering pachyderm that follows us around from room to room, the one's that's pushing me out of my own home, and the one that's blocking my view even as we speak.

TOM: It's just a word.

CHRISTINE: If only it were. (*Beat.*) Instead it's everything.

    (*Pause.*)

TOM: I've told you before, it's the only way.

CHRISTINE: It's your way. And it's a million miles from mine.

TOM: Is this how you want to be for the rest of your life…broken?

CHRISTINE: I don't have a choice.

TOM: Of course you damn well do!

CHRISTINE: I don't. It was taken away from me. He took it…on that day. And now I'm forever changed. And it doesn't matter what you say or what I do or how many years go by, it'll always be there…it's a permanent damage, Tom, whether you like it or not.

TOM: No one's saying it hasn't changed things – of course it's changed everything. But you've got to adapt to change. There is no other way.

CHRISTINE: Perhaps there isn't. But there is more than one way of adapting, and I don't know what the right way is, but it sure as hell isn't yours.

TOM: There is nothing wrong with forgiveness.

(CHRISTINE rises from the sofa and erupts with sudden fury.)

CHRISTINE: *There is when you're giving it to the man who murdered your own child!*

(Pause.)

TOM: (*Slowly and deliberately.*) It's not that simple.

CHRISTINE: How is it not that simple? This…this *thing* throttles the life out of your own flesh and blood, your own daughter, and all you do is turn around and say "That's okay."

TOM: I did *not* say that! You know damn well that's not what I said! I'm not excusing anything for God's sake!

CHRISTINE: What's the difference? Excusing, forgiving, it all amounts to the same thing at the end of the day, and I don't have it to give! Not now, not ever!

(*Pause.*)

TOM: You do. You just haven't found it yet.

CHRISTINE: What utter bullshit!

TOM: And I want you to, Christine. I need you to…for both our sakes.

CHRISTINE: Want me to find what? The ability to dismiss it all with a casual wave of the hand?

TOM: Oh, don't be so–

CHRISTINE: To smile benevolently and show the world what a remarkable generosity of spirit I possess?

TOM: Christine–

CHRISTINE: (*With increasing resentment.*) Because if it is, I don't have that kind of largesse. I don't have the kind of largesse that can see someone snuff out the life of my child and then shrug it off as if some guest at a dinner party had just broken another God damned wine glass!

TOM: That's enough!

(*Pause.*)

CHRISTINE: Did you love her?

(*Beat.*)

TOM: Don't you dare.

CHRISTINE: I'm just asking you a question.

TOM: *Don't*...you dare.

CHRISTINE: Because they'll all be asking it, you do know that, don't you? All of them. Friends, family, complete strangers.

TOM: Stop this now.

CHRISTINE: Not to your face, of course. To your face it'll be nothing but earnest looks of sympathy and carefully chosen words of condolence, all hoping not to sound as pat and clichéd as they inevitably will. But behind closed doors…they're sure to be wondering aloud. "Were they not close, do you suppose?" "Perhaps he was a distant father – not the paternal type?"

(*TOM crosses and confronts her.*)

TOM: Stop it!

CHRISTINE: Or even the grieving type, as I'm sure some of the less charitable will be raising their eyebrows and whispering, "That was quick."

(TOM *begins shaking her by the shoulders.*)

TOM: *I said stop it!*

(TOM *stops. Both freeze momentarily, the connotations of what just occurred lost on neither of them.*)

TOM: I'm sorry.

(TOM *removes his hands from her shoulders.*)

TOM: I'm so sorry.

(TOM *turns and crosses away from her. Pause.*)

TOM: You know damned well that I…that I loved that girl more than anything else in this world. Even more than you. (*Beat.*) You know I did. (*Beat.*) There was nothing I was more proud of than to have been a…a part of bringing her into this world…that…wonderful, beautiful person that she was. I suppose in some ways she…validated me. To have created something so…bright and full of life and hope amidst all the…well, all the rest of it. I suppose it made me feel that perhaps that was some kind of reason for it after all…or for me, at any rate. Because when you take a good, hard look at it all, it really doesn't amount to a whole lot. Not really. A job, a career…what does it all mean when all's said and done? What do you leave behind that couldn't have been done by someone else? But her…she did. She did mean something. And I don't have to justify myself or my reasoning to anybody. I don't care what they say or what they think. (*Beat.*) They'll do it anyway.

(*TOM crosses to the bar and pours himself another scotch.*)

TOM: Want one?

CHRISTINE: No. (*Beat.*) Yes.

(*TOM fixes her drink and crosses to hand it to her.*)

TOM: You see, it's all about perception, isn't it? That's what they say. People arrive at their conclusions based on a few…surface impressions of what they see before them. I say I forgive my daughter's killer for what he did, and they then perceive me to be cold and heartless. Or just plain bonkers. "Poor bastard, the shock of it must've pushed him off the edge." And what's to be done? I can't provide the accepted norms they want to see and hear…perceptions are formed…case – and minds – closed.

(*Pause.*)

CHRISTINE: I honestly don't give a shit what anyone else thinks.

TOM: Neither should you.

CHRISTINE: Only what you think.

TOM: You know what I think.

CHRISTINE: Yes, I do…and for the life of me I can't understand it. (*Beat.*) But I need to. I *have* to. She was ours, Tom. She was yours and mine. And I feel so dead inside…dead and empty. And sometimes I…I can barely breathe, and it's in my head and in my chest and in my lungs, and it all gets tighter and tighter and I just want it all to stop, I want it all to go away and just let me die…let me out of this. (*Beat.*) And then I see you…you, with all your calmness…your…your acceptance, and your… (*Beat.*) Forgiveness. (*Beat.*) And I hate you.

(*Pause.*)

TOM: What would you have me do?

(*Beat.*)

CHRISTINE: I don't know. (*Beat.*) Nothing. (*Beat.*) Explain. (*Beat.*) Explain how…I thought…after *all* those years…all of those years together…and then this happens and it's as if…I never knew you. Not the real one.

TOM: There's nothing to explain. Nothing I haven't already said. This is the way it must be.

CHRISTINE: No it isn't! (*Beat.*) This is the way you want it. But you live in a completely different world from me. You're somewhere else entirely. It's as if it all…washed over you somehow…as if you're not a part of it. But I can't escape it. It's all around me…all the time. And sometimes it's too much…I…I can't stand it…and I want it all to go away and never think of her again. Just not think of her, as if she'd never existed. If I could just erase her somehow. I know it's wrong, I know I shouldn't, but I can't help it…because it would all be so much easier. I could just be me again. (*Beat.*) But I can't. I can't escape. Every single day that I wake up, every room I walk into, all that I do reminds me of her. Everything here reminds me of her… (*Beat.*) Except you.

(*Pause.*)

TOM: We can't change what's happened. The only–

CHRISTINE: Christ almighty, will you stop with those tired bloody clichés every five fucking–

TOM: But it's the truth! The only thing we can control – or try to at least – is the aftermath. This. This is it. This is all we have. We can rage and hate for the rest of our lives, but it's not going to alter the fact that all we have is what's left behind.

(*Pause.*)

CHRISTINE: Yes…well, I don't want to be that.

TOM: Be what?

CHRISTINE: That which is left behind. The sad, tragic parent that buried her child, who must now struggle on to the end, martyred by her unbearable burden. The sort of person who friends quietly avoid so as to save themselves the embarrassment of not knowing what they should say. Someone whose name, when brought up in conversation, casts a sullen, piteous shadow over the proceedings, and then quickly passed over onto brighter, less troubling subjects. "Poor Christine…what's there to say?" (*Beat.*) That's what's left.

TOM: There is an alternative.

CHRISTINE: Oh, yes…the misunderstood saint.

TOM: How about the liberated survivor?

CHRISTINE: Christ, where do you pick up such crap? Oprah bloody Winfrey?

TOM: It isn't crap. If you'd only stop and think about it for a moment, you'd realize that it makes perfect sense.

CHRISTINE: What, "liberated survivor"? Do spare me, Tom. You make it sound as though you'd just staggered out of the gates of Auschwitz, not copped out on your daughter's death.

TOM: Copped out?

CHRISTINE: Or words to that effect. Pick something else – I don't care. All I know is that it'll take more than a few silly, pop-psych buzzwords to turn me into the kind of person who can so readily shirk their responsibilities.

TOM: Who's shirking anything?

CHRISTINE: You are.

TOM: By letting go of my anger?

CHRISTINE: By giving a free pass to the one person in this world I'd happily watch swinging from a gallows.

TOM: The only free pass being given out is the one I'm giving myself – the one that's giving me a chance to get past this and get my life back.

CHRISTINE: Well, how very kind of you. I hope you thanked you.

TOM: I deserve it and so do you.

CHRISTINE: And Susan?

TOM: Yes?

CHRISTINE: What does she get?

TOM: I'm...I don't follow.

CHRISTINE: Well, there are no more free passes left for her. Hers are all gone. So what does she get?

   (*Beat.*)

TOM: Our loving memory.

CHRISTINE: What a lousy consolation prize.

TOM: It's all we have.

CHRISTINE: What about respect? What about *respecting* her memory?

TOM: I am. I do.

CHRISTINE: By doing that?

TOM: By letting go.

CHRISTINE: Of her.

TOM: No, no, not–

CHRISTINE: Of all she was. Of what she meant. (*Beat.*) To us. (*Beat.*) To me.

TOM: There is nothing disrespectful to Susan in us trying to get on with our lives.

CHRISTINE: At her expense.

TOM: No, of course not.

CHRISTINE: It's a slap in the face.

TOM: It's a *way out*. A way to free yourself from this.

CHRISTINE: No, let's call it by its proper name, shall we? (*Beat.*) It's a betrayal.

TOM: *What?*

CHRISTINE: A betrayal. A betrayal of me, a betrayal of us, and most unconscionably of all, it's a betrayal of Susan.

TOM: How could you possibly–

CHRISTINE: You stabbed me in the back, you spat on her grave, and you did it all on cue.

TOM: How can you even think such things, let alone–

CHRISTINE: When you stood in front of those reporters with your head held oh-so-high, telling them in soft, compassionate tones of how you'd found it within yourself to forgive that *thing* for what he'd done, you very calmly, very magnanimously, and very publicly betrayed us all. (*Beat.*) I'm glad it's helped you find peace.

TOM: That's a very ugly word, Christine.

CHRISTINE: It's an ugly act.

TOM: I wish you hadn't used it.

CHRISTINE: I wish you hadn't done it.

TOM: *Done what? Done what, for Christ's sake?* (*Beat.*) We had reporters camped outside of here day and night and they weren't going anywhere until they'd got a statement. One of us had to do something.

CHRISTINE: You could have just said, "No comment."

TOM: And there they would have stayed.

CHRISTINE: Then you should have said the usual claptrap people say in these situations. They eat it up, no matter how many times they've heard it before.

TOM: I said what I felt.

CHRISTINE: It was private.

TOM: I told the truth.

CHRISTINE: *You should have lied!*

TOM: Why? Why on earth would I do that?

CHRISTINE: Because it was private! It was between you and me. It was *our* business – *our* dirty business. As if it wasn't bad enough being knocked sideways when you told *me* you'd let that creature off the hook, you then decide to double down by telling the whole God damned world you had!

TOM: No one's letting anyone off the hook. Just because I forgive him, it doesn't make him any less culpable.

    (*Pause.*)

CHRISTINE: Why did you leave me there?

TOM: What do you mean?

CHRISTINE: On the doorstep. Why did you leave me standing there…alone?

TOM: I…I thought you might have something to say yourself.

CHRISTINE: So you left?

TOM: Yes, I, I…thought you might…feel more comfortable without me there.

CHRISTINE: Comfortable? Standing alone on the doorstep in front of all those vultures, shoving their microphones in my face? No…no, I can't say I felt very comfortable, Tom.

    (*CHRISTINE moves downstage, gazing off into the distance. Pause.*)

CHRISTINE: I just stared at them. I stood there…and just stared. Quite expressionless. Saying nothing. There was lots I could have said, of course. Lots and lots. Some of it would probably have made a lot of people hate me. But I just stared at them. (*Beat.*) "How are you handling all of this, Mrs. Wilkes?" Do *you* forgive your daughter's killer, Mrs. Wilkes?" "How did you and your husband manage to find forgiveness for such a heinous act?" "Do you think Susan would be proud of you?" (*Pause.*) I just stared. (*Beat.*) Then came back inside.

(*Pause.*)

TOM: I'm sorry, I…I should have waited. I wasn't thinking.

CHRISTINE: Not about me, at least.

TOM: I…I suppose I thought you'd follow.

CHRISTINE: Dutifully?

TOM: I just wanted to get away from them.

CHRISTINE: Did you? Did you really? I think you rather enjoyed it.

TOM: What? Oh, don't be preposterous!

CHRISTINE: I do. I think you rather liked it.

TOM: It had to be done.

CHRISTINE: Your little fifteen minutes of fame.

TOM: You must be kidding?

CHRISTINE: Why not? Everyone's doing it these days.

TOM: This is silly.

CHRISTINE: Is it? I wonder.

TOM: And quite offensive, actually.

CHRISTINE: Well, you'd know more about that than me.

TOM: I have absolutely no interest in–

CHRISTINE: They say it's like a drug – once you get a taste for it, you know…it's never enough.

TOM: What *are* you talking about?

(*CHRISTINE moves to the bar and refills her glass.*)

CHRISTINE: And it's a catchy angle – I can see the appeal. "Promising young student assaulted and slain in her own flat, yet father of murder victim somehow finds love in his heart for daughter's killer." Who wouldn't click on that? Surely worth a quick glance? And before you know it, you're a minor, temporary celebrity.

TOM: Have you finished?

CHRISTINE: Almost. (*Beat.*) So our minor, temporary celebrity, sensing that his flickering glimmer of attention is about to be extinguished by the brutality of life in the twenty-four hour news cycle, decides to write a quick book about his experience. A self-help book, marketed towards those who've experienced the garrotting of a loved one, those who've simply experienced loss and grief, and, to ensure a healthy profit margin, the just plain prurient.

TOM: What nonsense are you talking about? What book? I'm not writing any book.

CHRISTINE: Well, I think you should. I think you should capitalize on your new found fame before you become yesterday's news…which probably already happened…yesterday.

TOM: This is ridiculous.

CHRISTINE: Very…but that's celebrity. Comes with the territory. Still, I'm sure you'll get used to it. And let's face it, there's something vaguely ridiculous about making a career out of being a career guidance counselor, isn't there? I mean, basic logic dictates you'd have to have had one to guide one.

TOM: Now you're just being nasty.

CHRISTINE: Not at all. I'm just suggesting that your transition into celebrityhood may not be quite the wrenching experience you imagine it to be.

TOM: If anyone's imagining things here it's you. Look, I did not enjoy speaking to those people, I have no intention of writing any book about anything at anytime, and I find it insulting in the extreme that you should imply that I find anything pleasurable about any aspect of this…wholly lamentable situation.

CHRISTINE: "Wholly lamentable." What a very nice way of putting it. How very English.

(Beat.)

TOM: Painful, then.

CHRISTINE: I'll write the forward, if you like. As long as you promise not to censor me. *(Beat.)* Let's see, how would I begin… *(Beat.)* Well, how about…"When my husband first called me at the school to inform me…oh, I suppose I should mention that I'm a teacher by profession – English, French, when called upon, and, uh…manners – the latter I'm not paid for, of course, but strictly enforce anyway. Anyway, when my husband called me to inform me that our daughter had been murdered – strangled to death – by an up-and-coming serial killer…though I'm not sure if three makes you up-and-coming or having arrived, but three it was…I thought…well, actually, I didn't think anything. My mind just sort of stopped. There was too much to compute, I suppose. Too out of the ordinary. Was it a joke? Was it really him? He would never do something like that as a joke. He would never do something like that, full stop. And where would be the joke in it? Was I imagining it? Imagining I'm on the phone with my husband, and he's telling me my daughter's dead? A day dream I was having that's suddenly gotten out of hand? Everything stopped. Nothing was real. The room began to move around me. Who was this person on the phone? When would I wake up? (*Pause.*) The…*creature*…the "person" in question, was, as it turns out, a product of Sierra Leone, who'd slithered his way to Europe, snuck past border enforcement at Calais, and arrived in England with no money, little education, and a very strong pair of hands. He also, we later learned, was in possession of a highly-charged libido that found immense satisfaction in coitus post-mortem…or fucking the dead, if you prefer. All of this, naturally, I found quite disturbing. (*Beat.*) My husband, on the other hand–

TOM: All right, that's enough.

CHRISTINE: *No!* (*Beat.*) No censoring. (*Beat.*) Not anymore.

TOM: Why do you want to go over–

CHRISTINE: Because it's my turn now, that's why! You had yours with the reporters, now I'm having mine with you.

(TOM *takes a breath, crosses to the bar and refills his glass. Pause.*)

CHRISTINE: So…when it had sunk in and, uh…well…sunk

me…I turned, dependently…needily, even…to my husband, the kindly career guidance counselor, seeking, I suppose…a little guidance. Somehow I imagined that together we'd find some way of…grappling with it…sharing our grief…our loss…getting through it. (*Beat.*) But…much to my surprise, he wasn't there. It wasn't him. Just like on the phone that fatal day, when I thought it wasn't really him. Only this time it really wasn't. He'd become someone else. Someone I didn't know. Someone who walked around with a beneficent smirk on their face, and who suddenly seemed oblivious to the fact that their very own child had been raped and brutally murdered…though not necessarily in that order.

TOM: I really don't think this is a good idea. I really think that–

CHRISTINE: Susan's face–

TOM: Christine, please–

CHRISTINE: *Susan's face*…on the other hand, did not wear a beneficent smile, as one might expect. When we were called in to identify her, it was…well, frankly something of a guessing game, in as much as it sort of looked like her, but really could have been anyone. Hard to look at if it had been a complete stranger, let alone your own daughter. It was beaten black and blue, the jaw broken and hanging unnaturally to one side, teeth broken, nose broken, eyes swollen and bulging. The official cause of death was strangulation, but it remains unknown whether the aforementioned injuries occurred before, during, or after the asphyxiation…or the screwing.

TOM: That's enough!

CHRISTINE: *No!*

TOM: Why are you doing this?

CHRISTINE: It's a foreword – a foreword. They help provide context and that's what I'm giving it!

TOM: We both know the context. We've both lived it, for Christ's sake.

CHRISTINE: One of us has.

TOM: We *both* have.

CHRISTINE: And so when my husband came to me on that very surreal morning and told me that he'd forgiven the creature from the Congo – or rather, Sierra Leone – well, I…I just sort of looked at him in bemusement. It was if he were speaking another language. Congolese, perhaps? Or whatever they speak in Sierra Leone…which may also be Congolese for all I know…or care. All I knew was that my big-hearted, beneficent, altruistic, kind and philanthropic husband had somehow managed to find it within himself to forgive the unforgivable. So large was his largesse, that even the rape and butchering of his one and only offspring wasn't sufficient to derail the exoneration express as it chugged its way to Never Never Land…or Never Never Mind, one might say.

TOM: I think that's enough, don't you? I think you've had your turn.

CHRISTINE: Just…just the conclusion…to my foreword… (*Beat.*) So…in conclusion…as you wend your way through the God knows how many pages of this self-aggrandizing, limp, meaningless piece of life-affirming crap, I do hope that you'll keep one foot on the ground, an eye to the truth, and…and an understanding that however *nice* you like to think you are, or wish you were, or aspire to be, there are some things…some things that just cannot be pardoned.

(*Pause.*)

TOM: Have you finished now?

CHRISTINE: Yes…yes, I've finished now.

TOM: And we're back on planet earth, are we?

CHRISTINE: One of us never left.

(*Pause.*)

TOM: Christine, look, I know this has been…unbearable…to say the very least. I know things will never be the same again – for either of us. And I know that however hard we try, there will be countless times in the future when we'll break down all over again…as if for the first time.

CHRISTINE: Or *even* the first time.

TOM: Can I speak?

(*CHRISTINE turns away dismissively.*)

TOM: It'll always be with us. She'll always be with us and what happened will always be with us. We don't have a choice in that. But we do have a choice in what happens next…in what we make of the rest of it. (*Beat.*) You claim there's not much there worth salvaging. That it's not worth the effort. That from hereon everything is wrong. But I don't agree. (*Beat.*) Life isn't over, even if it seems like it is. Ours go on. And we can either fold our hand and quit the game, or we can play the cards we've got left to the best of our ability.

(*Beat.*)

CHRISTINE: If only we were playing the same game.

TOM: We are…we're just playing by different rules.

CHRISTINE: I don't like your rules.

TOM: I'm not asking you to like them…just try them.

CHRISTINE: I think I'd choke on them. (*Beat.*) No pun intended.

(*Pause.*)

TOM: Let me ask you something. If you're so consumed with anger and hatred for this young man, then why would–

CHRISTINE: Young man? *Young man?* Good God, you make him sound almost human – almost one of us – as if he were about to enter prep school or shave for the very first time. (*Scoffing.*) Young man!

TOM: All right then, creature. If it makes you feel better, creature. If this creature fills your being with such loathing, why on earth are you allowing him to kill for the second time?

CHRISTINE: Susan was the third.

TOM: All right, fourth, fourth! I'm talking about you.

CHRISTINE: Me?

TOM: Yes, you. You're allowing him to kill you, too. You've already said as much. You've said you're dead inside. Dead because of what's happened. Dead because of what he did to Susan. If you really hated him that much, you wouldn't let him do that. You wouldn't let him destroy you, too. You wouldn't give him that satisfaction.

(Pause.)

CHRISTINE: Nice try.

TOM: What do you mean, "Nice try"? I'm not *trying* anything, I'm just pointing out a simple fact.

CHRISTINE: Yes, very. Very simple, actually. Well-intentioned, I'm sure, but very simplistic, nonetheless.

TOM: Are you even listening?

CHRISTINE: It would read well, though. You should use it in the book.

TOM: For Christ's sake, will you just shut up about this God damned book!

(Pause.)

CHRISTINE: He killed me when he killed Susan. He's already won.

TOM: Well, that's strange, because you look very much alive from where I'm standing.

CHRISTINE: It's an illusion.

TOM: And he's only won if you decide to let him.

CHRISTINE: Tom, I don't care, don't you understand? I don't care who's won and who's lost. It's over for Susan and it's over for us. Whatever you and I were or weren't, none of it matters now. Whatever we'd become…had…slid into, was always tacitly acceptable because of Susan. Whatever we'd lost along the way, she was always the piece that kept it working. She was our excuse. (*Beat.*) But now we don't have one.

   (*Pause.*)

TOM: I'm sorry you see it that way. I've never needed an excuse to be with you. It's just always been something that I wanted…needed. I know things haven't always been perfect. I'm certainly not perfect, and neither are you. No one is, and if you think they exist you'll never find them. But all in all, I think you and I got pretty damned lucky in finding each other, even if you don't think so. And despite all of your protestations and claims that I live in some dream world and that you're the one who faces life head-on, never afraid to confront reality, I do think that in this instance…in regard to you and I and our life together, such as it is…that it's you who's the one hiding from the truth.

   (*Pause.*)

CHRISTINE: The truth? (*Beat.*) The truth is, I…I truly wish I could feel that…believe in it…hold onto it somehow. Part of me wants to. I…almost can. (*Beat.*) But it's just that…almost. I wish it weren't…but it is. Because it's a mirage. Unreachable. I see it…shimmering off in the distance, but I know it's not really there. It looks nice…quite comforting…but it's a trick. Because the closer I get the less I recognize it. Because it's not really you. (*Beat.*) Not anymore.

(*Beat.*)

TOM: Then tell me...what can I do to reach...to make it not almost?

(*Beat.*)

CHRISTINE: You already know. (*Beat.*) Not forgive.

TOM: But I...I can't do that, Christine. If I don't...how can I carry on?

CHRISTINE: The same as me.

TOM: But you're not.

CHRISTINE: Yes, I am...just not like before.

TOM: Nothing can be like it was before, that's the whole point.

CHRISTINE: Yes...but your before and after are entirely different to mine.

TOM: No they're not. Really, they're not. It's just a question of perspective. There a bigger picture here. Much bigger. If you'd only been there and seen him, you'd...

(*Pause.*)

CHRISTINE: What?

(*Pause.*)

CHRISTINE: What did you just say?

(*Pause.*)

TOM: I…I meant to tell you. I… (*Beat.*) I saw him.

(*Pause.*)

CHRISTINE: You saw him?

(*Beat.*)

TOM: Yes, I…I went to see him…in the prison.

(*Pause.*)

CHRISTINE: When?

(*Beat.*)

TOM: Yesterday.

(*Pause.*)

CHRISTINE: (*Closing her eyes and turning away.*) I see.

(*Pause.*)

TOM: Honestly, I did…I meant to tell you before, but it…I didn't know how. It's not exactly something you can…just drop into conversation. (*Beat.*) I know…I know it's important, but…well, with you…the way you are, I…I just wasn't sure when to—

CHRISTINE: (*Erupting in fury.*) *Why?*

TOM: Because I...I needed to.

CHRISTINE: (*Unrelenting.*) *Why?*

TOM: Because I needed to...see him, to face him, to...to make it...real, I suppose.

(*Pause.*)

CHRISTINE: God, I feel sick.

TOM: Christine, listen to me, you know I couldn't have told you before, you know I couldn't. It was something I had to do for me, and had to do whether you liked it or not. You know as well as I do that—

CHRISTINE: *"Liked it"?* Did you just say *"liked it"?*

TOM: Then, no, accepted – accepted it.

(*Beat.*)

CHRISTINE: Accepted *what?* What, exactly? That you took time out of your day to go and spend some quality time with some Sub-Saharan monster that raped and mutilated our daughter? What on earth would give you the impression that I might be upset about that? No, no, I think it's very thoughtful of you. I think every mother of a corpse would feel exactly the same way.

TOM: I'm sorry I didn't tell you before I went, but you know very well why I couldn't.

CHRISTINE: How's he doing, by the way? Is he eating enough?

TOM: Christine–

CHRISTINE: Hopefully you took him a few treats to help take his mind off things. It must be so difficult for him.

TOM: Can we please talk sensibly?

CHRISTINE: Oh, I am, I am. Perhaps I'll stop by tomorrow and drop him off a nice homemade cake or something – help perk up his spirits.

TOM: Christine, I needed to see him, I needed to see who he was. I needed to fill in the missing pieces in my head. I couldn't spend the rest of my life just imagining…it…all of it. I just couldn't.

   (Pause.)

CHRISTINE: And?

TOM: And what?

CHRISTINE: What did you find? What did your little human safari reveal to you? Did it put your already anesthetized mind on a more relaxed footing, or did you find yourself mildly disturbed by the true extent of your own hypocrisy?

TOM: I found…what I was looking for, I think.

CHRISTINE: Sainthood?

TOM: No…I found – as you might say – some context. Something to…frame it all in.

CHRISTINE: Oh, how very lovely for you.

TOM: It actually helped a great deal.

CHRISTINE: The visit?

TOM: Yes.

CHRISTINE: You or him?

TOM: Me, of course.

CHRISTINE: Why "of course"? It was a perfectly legitimate question. I mean, one minute you're forgiving him, the next you're bonding with him. Where does it end? Perhaps we should rewrite our will? Create a foundation in his name? Campaign for early parole? (*Beat.*) *I mean, what in God's name is wrong with you?*

(*Pause.*)

TOM: No one was bonding with anyone. (*Beat.*) I went there to…to try to make some sense out of the nonsensical. To get some kind of… meaning …where none existed. (*Beat.*) I'm a pretty logical person by nature. You know this. You don't always like it, but it's the way I am. I'm also aware that…some things happen in life that don't make a whole lot of sense, no matter how much you wish they did. A cable snaps, a computer malfunctions, a car skids…all sorts of little ways for great tragedies to be wrought that don't give us the comfort of reason. They just happen. A life is lost and shockwaves reverberate around those left behind until the end, all wondering why? Why them? Why their daughter? Their son? Mother? (*Beat.*) But I'm not good with random, with chance, with all that being in the wrong place at the wrong time stuff. Some people are. Some people can chalk it up to some sort of existential, incomprehensible mad bit of bad luck in a grand scheme they know nothing of, however great their pain. Some find solace in placing the responsibility in the lap of God, his reasoning being mysterious but absolute. But none of that works for me. (*Beat.*) I needed some form of accounting, even if the facts – the horror of the facts – told me there could be none. And so I decided I would have to see this person for myself, to see if perhaps, in seeing him, in meeting him, I could…I could discover, take away, something, anything that would…show me some kind of cause. (*Beat.*) And…to some degree…it did.

(*Pause.*)

CHRISTINE: There is nothing on this earth that could ever justify what that girl went through. To suggest that there is, is just plain delusional. Perhaps even hysterical. (*Beat.*) Certainly cruel.

(*Pause.*)

TOM: He was born in 1985 in a village about an hour outside of Freetown, Sierra Leone's capital. By the time the war in neighboring Liberia had spilled over into Sierra Leone several years later, he'd already lost his mother to AIDS, and his father had simply disappeared one day, with no one knowing his exact fate. He had two brothers and three sisters. They raised themselves from that point on, the eldest sister, aged ten at the time, being the matriarch. By 1998, the country's civil war had reached their village. It was burned to the ground. All of the women and older people who hadn't fled were either raped or butchered or both. The children were taken to camps where the pro-government militia that had brought about this carnage taught them to fight and kill. They were conditioned with marijuana, cocaine, and other locally concocted barbiturates in order to numb them to what they would be forced to do. In their training, this sometimes included slitting the throat or shooting, execution-style, someone from the village they'd grown up with.

(Pause.)

CHRISTINE: Quite the little chatterbox, wasn't he. Sounds like you two got on like a house on fire.

TOM: I never spoke with him, Christine. It wasn't permitted. I was only allowed to view him very briefly through a small observation pane in the door of his cell. And only then at my insistence…or perhaps pleading would be more accurate…and a little bribing. Everything I'm telling you was told to me by his caseworker.

CHRISTINE: Just as well, I'd imagine – unless you've been studying the languages of the Dark Continent on the sly.

TOM: Not that it matters, but actually, English is the official language of Sierra Leone. I'd have thought you'd have known that.

(Beat.)

CHRISTINE: Were I a geography teacher, then doubtless I would.

TOM: Anyway… *(Beat.)* In 2002, when the civil war had officially ended, he, at the grand old age of seventeen, sought to escape all of the horror and obscenity that he'd seen and committed, and so made his way to a refugee camp in Guinea. From there he eventually made it to France, to Calais, and ultimately to England, equipped with little more than a scarred mind and a drug habit, and…a desire for a better life, one assumes. Unfortunately, it didn't turn out that way.

(Beat.)

CHRISTINE: Unfortunately for whom, Tom?

(Beat.)

TOM: For all of us.

CHRISTINE: Jesus! There's no end to you, is there?

TOM: Christine, we're all a part of this, don't you see? It's not his village or our city, it's…it's all connected. We live in *our* house on *our* street in *our* country, and we find a thousand different ways to define who we are and differentiate ourselves from others. We read about something happening in another country and it might as well be happening on another planet. But it's make believe…something we've created ourselves to make us feel safe and apart from all of the world's horrors. The truth is we're *one* group of people on *one* planet, and sometimes our lives interconnect in ways you could never imagine. Histories catch up. And in this instance…well, it's all one great big, mutual, horrible…tragedy.

(Pause.)

CHRISTINE: No it isn't. We weren't a part of that. We're not to blame for what happened to him or his family or his village. It had nothing to do with us. This is beyond excuses, there is no justification. This was a ruthless, savage act by a ruthless, savage person, and it was perpetrated upon our daughter, who was as loving and caring a person you could ever hope to meet. If a civil war in Africa is all it takes to put your heart and mind at rest, then I'm glad for you. (*Beat.*) Me? I just miss her.

TOM: It's not justification, it's an explanation. Christ, you were the one talking about context – this is bloody context! This is it! Doesn't that mean anything to you? Doesn't it help you make some kind of sense of what happened?

CHRISTINE: It helps explain how he became a monster…nothing more.

TOM: And that doesn't help you on some level?

CHRISTINE: Why would it?

TOM: Because…because suddenly it's not random. It's not random. It's no longer some inexplicable, irrational act. It's…it makes some sense at last.

CHRISTINE: I see, it makes sense now, does it?

TOM: No…no, not like that. Not in the way you mean. But it…there's dots to connect. There's some structure, some…framework that links it all together.

(*Beat.*)

CHRISTINE: What possible solace do you think I could find in knowing that animal's grotesque backstory? If those people choose to behave like savages, tearing each other apart in unspeakable ways, then that's their business. It's their country, it's their life, it's of their choosing, so let them get on with it. Here things are different. We're not one world – we're all different and we have different values. That's why we have borders and immigration control, and if they'd only worked better, Susan would still be alive and that *thing* would still be crawling around in that rathole of a country it came from.

TOM: I'm not talking about borders or values or ways of life, I'm simply–

CHRISTINE: Yes you are. Just a second ago you were prattling on about how we were all part of some glorious global village, where we're all one great big, interconnected happy family. Well, we're not and we never will be. And neither should we be. And if you want to know why, then ask your daughter.

(*Beat.*)

TOM: Can you not just see that all of this...that it has some kind of rationale now?

CHRISTINE: No, I can't. All I know is that Susan is dead, some alleged life-form is behind bars, and that you have decided to crown yourself the next Mother Teresa...or Judas, depending upon your point of view.

TOM: Christine, you've got to stop this. You've got to...get that poison out of you head, to try to find an alternative to this. There is a reason that this happened. It isn't right, it isn't fair, it isn't how it should have been. It's ugly and horrible and unthinkable. But it happened. (*Beat.*) Now, we can silently scream at the injustice of it all until the day we die, or we can try to come to some kind of terms with it. Try to somehow, despite the weight of our grief, make it something tangible...and consequently bearable. Susan's death...it's beyond comprehension on our terms. But if you read the small print...if you really study it... (*Beat.*) Well...there's some comfort there. There is, really.

(*Beat.*)

CHRISTINE: Comfort?

TOM: All right, then...closure.

CHRISTINE: (*With a mocking laugh.*) *Closure*? What the hell is that? What daytime show are you quoting now, Dr. Wilkes?

TOM: It's a word...one with meaning. You should think about it.

CHRISTINE: There's no such thing. It's one of those stupid terms made up to make stupid people feel clever.

TOM: I believe in it.

CHRISTINE: Well, you just keep on doing that.

(*Beat.*)

TOM: I have to.

(*Pause.*)

CHRISTINE: And what are you looking for now?

(*Beat.*)

TOM: I'm...I don't understand.

CHRISTINE: I'm asking what you're looking for. What do you want? My acceptance of all this? An excuse for him? An excuse for you? I'm asking you...what did you hope to achieve by going there, by...looking at...*it*?

(*Beat.*)

TOM: Like I said...to complete a picture. I needed an answer.

CHRISTINE: To what?

TOM: To murder.

(*Pause.*)

CHRISTINE: Yes. (*Beat.*) And there's where we part. There's where the road forks. Because I cannot now – and never will – find any so-called answers that could ever put my demons to rest. No supposed logic you've found in any of this will ever act as some sort of cheap balm for my mind or my heart. They're seared with grief and hatred, and if they weren't I think I'd probably stop breathing.

(*CHRISTINE buries her face in her hands.*)

TOM: Oh, God.

(*Pause.*)

TOM: Can I...hold you?

(*Beat.*)

CHRISTINE: No.

(*Pause.*)

TOM: What can I do? (*Beat.*) I don't know what to do. I don't know how to get through to you…to…help you.

(*Beat.*)

CHRISTINE: You know damned well.

(*Beat.*)

TOM: Aside from that.

CHRISTINE: That's it.

TOM: You know I can't.

CHRISTINE: Won't.

TOM: I *can't*. (*Beat.*) I *can't* not forgive.

CHRISTINE: It's a choice. You choose not to. Therefore you won't.

TOM: It's not a choice for me, Christine, don't you get it? It's not an option. If I…if I put myself where you are, I don't think I could…I think I'd…

CHRISTINE: Show some emotion?

(*Pause.*)

TOM: Why must you do that?

CHRISTINE: Do what?

TOM: Say such things.

CHRISTINE: It was fair comment.

TOM: It was hurtful.

CHRISTINE: It was fair comment.

(*Beat.*)

TOM: Do you like this?

CHRISTINE: What?

TOM: This. Hurting me. Does it make you feel better?

CHRISTINE: No, Tom. (*Beat.*) What I *like*...is to see emotional responses to emotional situations. That's what I *like*.

TOM: Doesn't that amount to the same thing?

CHRISTINE: Not where you're concerned, it doesn't.

TOM: I'm not with you.

CHRISTINE: I think we've established that.

TOM: But what are you saying?

CHRISTINE: If it doesn't hurt, how can you feel it? Or vice versa.

(*Beat.*)

TOM: Are you saying...that this hasn't hurt me? Are you...questioning my feelings? (*Beat.*) Are you?

CHRISTINE: How could I? I've never seen them.

(*Beat.*)

TOM: My God, you've got some nerve. I'm beginning to wonder if you really are dead inside after all.

CHRISTINE: If I am, I wonder what that would make you.

TOM: It makes me in control of the situation, that's what! Jesus Christ, what would you have me do, stomp around in here, bawling at the top of my lungs every five minutes? Flail around like some helpless sad-sack, endlessly ranting and raving at the terrible injustice of it all? Is that what you want? Is it?

CHRISTINE: What I would–

TOM: Perhaps we should do it together, the two of us in unison, destroying ourselves in one great big orgy of self-flagellating misery! Now, wouldn't that be a sight?

(*CHRISTINE crosses over to him confrontationally.*)

CHRISTINE: What I would like to see from you...

TOM: Yes?

CHRISTINE: Just once, just for *once*...

TOM: I'm listening.

CHRISTINE: (*Slowly and deliberately.*) Is…some…*anger.*

(*Beat.*)

TOM: For what purpose?

CHRISTINE: (*Almost hissing.*) For *me*…that's for what purpose.

(*Beat.*)

TOM: It doesn't help.

CHRISTINE: It would help *me*.

TOM: It's destructive…self-destructive.

CHRISTINE: No it isn't.

TOM: I assure you it is. You probably can't realize that now because you're–

CHRISTINE: I'll tell you exactly what it is – it's a *normal…human…reaction.*

TOM: All it does is cause more–

CHRISTINE: A *normal…human…reaction.*

TOM: What good could there possibly be–

CHRISTINE: (*Increasingly agitated.*) Right from the beginning, right from the very start of this whole nightmare, I've seen you nothing but calm, collected and in control. From the first grave but calm call when you told me what had happened, to your stoicism and composure when we saw her in the morgue, to your forgiving and understanding and informing the press of your inner peace now that you'd reconciled everything in your heart, and it's all so bloody lovely and magnanimous and peaceful and calm *but none of it's real!*

(*Beat.*)

TOM: It's just a different way of–

CHRISTINE: *It's not! It's not real! It's not normal!*

TOM: It is for me.

CHRISTINE: *It isn't!* (*Bellowing.*) *Your daughter is dead! Why can't you be angry!*

TOM: Because I will *not* allow–

CHRISTINE: (*With mounting hysteria.*) What do I have to do, huh? Tell me! What do I have to do to make you angry? Hmm? Hit you? Would that do it?

(*CHRISTINE begins slapping TOM about his head and body.*)

TOM: Stop it!

CHRISTINE: Push you around? Slap you around a bit?

TOM: For God's sake!

CHRISTINE: Throw things at you? Will that do it?

(CHRISTINE *begins picking up anything at hand and throwing it at him.*)

TOM: Christine!

CHRISTINE: Does it? Does it? What do I have to do? Tell me? Break all your…this shit?

(CHRISTINE *begins smashing barware, pictures, anything she finds, throwing it on the floor and across the room.*)

CHRISTINE: Break all this shit? How does that feel? And this? And this? Tell me! Tell me!

TOM: For God's sake pull yourself together!

(CHRISTINE *grabs the photograph of Susan from the sideboard.*)

CHRISTINE: Or this? What about this?

TOM: *No!*

CHRISTINE: *Yes!*

(CHRISTINE *hurls the picture across the room, smashing it to pieces. She briefly stares at the spot where it landed, before covering her head with her arms.*)

CHRISTINE: Tell me what I have to do.

(CHRISTINE *slumps onto the sofa, crying.*)

CHRISTINE: What do I have to do? (*Beat.*) What do I have to do?

(*There is a long pause. Eventually* TOM *crosses over to the sofa and sits down next to – but apart from –* CHRISTINE. *After several moments, he takes a deep breath before speaking.*)

TOM: I'm…sure that you already know this, but…when the human body is…injured in some way, some quite painful way…it releases endorphins into its system in order to numb itself to that which…might otherwise be unbearable. It creates its own opiate to drug itself into tolerating the intolerable. It's how it survives…or tries to. (*Pause.*) When the police first arrived at my office to…to inform me, consolingly but also quite…bluntly, of what had happened to Susan, I…well, I don't know how to describe it, quite honestly. Initially I…I didn't believe them, it just didn't seem…possible. I thought there must have been some sort of mistake. I told them as much. (*Beat.*) They…assured me that there was no mistake…that identification had been found on her body and…that they were…well, very sorry. (*Beat.*) After they left, I…it didn't so much sink in as…envelop me. Entirely. I wanted to scream. Every part of my body wanted to scream. I thought I would explode. It was too much to take in, to contain. I wanted to scream so loudly that the sheer force of my voice would…make it not true. That I could stop it. (*Beat.*) But I couldn't. I couldn't stop it. And I couldn't scream. (*Beat.*) Instead, this…strange feeling swept over me. Over my mind. Over everything. It was almost physical. I felt it hit me, roll right over me. It hit so hard I thought I would faint. It was like being drunk. Too drunk. Everything was in slow motion, and I was falling… (*Beat.*) And then I was numb. And I think I knew why…in a way. But it didn't matter, because I couldn't control it. It all just sort of shut down…because it had to. But it was okay, you see, because it made it…because…I could breathe again. It suddenly all looked different. It was apart from me. (*Placing his fist against his chest.*) It wasn't in here anymore. It was somewhere else. And so was I. (*Beat.*) And there I've been ever since…hiding…scared…in this…strange calm. Scared but protected…from all that would consume me…submerge me. I'm on an island, you see? And it's very small…and it's very lonely. (*Beat.*) And I can't get off it. (*Beat.*) Not yet. (*As he begins to cry.*) And this is how I survive. And I know it may seem cowardly…but it's what I must do. I know there are storms and raging seas all around me, but…but here…here on my island, if I look up at the sky…it's blue and it's calm…and it's safe. And if I just keep looking up…then the rest of it…I can let go of. (*Pause.*) Please forgive me.

(*After some time, CHRISTINE slowly gets to her feet and picks up the suitcase.*)

TOM: Where are you going?

(*Pause.*)

CHRISTINE: Upstairs…to put these back where they belong.

(*CHRISTINE begins to cross towards the door.*)

TOM: Thank you.

(*CHRISTINE stops and turns back to face him.*)

CHRISTINE: They're not mine. They're hers. (*Beat.*) A few things she'd left behind. I'd decided to get rid of them, but… (*Beat.*) Well, I've…changed my mind.

(*Pause.*)

TOM: Thank you.

(*CHRISTINE makes to leave again. Before she exits, TOM calls out to her.*)

TOM: Christine.

(*CHRISTINE stops in the doorway and looks back.*)

TOM: Will you…could you…hold me?

(*Pause.*)

CHRISTINE: No. (*Pause.*) Not yet.

(*TOM gives a small nod of understanding as CHRISTINE exits. He turns back around and stares up into space as the lights fade down to BLACK.*)

END OF PLAY

ABOUT THE AUTHOR

From the Royal Court Theatre in London to the Playhouse Theatre in Tasmania, the works of award-winning playwright Andrew Biss have been performed across the globe, spanning four continents. His plays have won awards on both coasts of the U.S., critical acclaim in the U.K., and quickly became a perennial sight on Off and Off-Off Broadway stages.

In London his plays have been performed at The Royal Court Theatre, Theatre503, Riverside Studios, The Pleasance Theatre, The Union Theatre, The White Bear Theatre, The Brockley Jack Studio Theatre, Fractured Lines Theatre & Film at COG ARTSpace, and Ghost Dog Productions at The Horse & Stables.

In New York his plays have been produced at Theatre Row Studios, The Samuel French Off-Off-Broadway Festival, The Kraine Theater, The Red Room Theater, Times Square Arts Center, Manhattan Theatre Source, Mind The Gap Theatre, 3Graces Theatre Company, Emerging Artists Theatre, Curan Repertory Company, Pulse Ensemble Theatre, American Globe Theatre, The American Theater of Actors, and Chashama Theatres, among others.

His plays and monologues are published in numerous anthologies from trade publishers Bedford/St. Martin's, Smith & Kraus, Inc., Pioneer Drama Service, and Applause Theatre & Cinema Books.

Andrew is a graduate of the University of the Arts London, and a member of the Dramatists Guild of America, Inc.

For more information please visit his website at:

www.andrewbiss.com

ADDITIONAL SELECTED TITLES
BY THIS AUTHOR

The End of the World

5M/3F Approx. 90 minutes

Valentine's parents have decided that the time has finally come for their son to leave home and discover life for himself. As he ventures forth into the vast world beyond, his new adventure is soon drawn to a halt when he is mugged at gunpoint. Frightened and exhausted, he seeks shelter at a bed and breakfast establishment named The End of the World, run by the dour Mrs. Anna. Here Valentine encounters a Bosnian woman with a hole where her stomach used to be, an American entrepreneur with a scheme to implant televisions into people's foreheads, and a Catholic priest who attempts to lure him down inside a kitchen sink. Then things start getting strange...

In this story based loosely around the state of Bardo from The Tibetan Book of the Dead - an intermediate state where the dead arrive prior to rebirth - dying is the easy part. Getting out of Bardo and returning to the land of the living is a far more perilous proposition, and unless you know what you're doing...you might never leave.

An odd, yet oddly touching tale of life, death, and the space in-between.

Leah's Gals

3M/5F Approx. 90 minutes

Leah's just won the lottery in what she describes as "the biggest single, one-time cash haul in this here dirt-poor, shitty state's history!" But, rather than living the highlife, Leah decides to split the winnings among her three daughters, asking only for a deathbed-style declaration of love in return. When her youngest daughter, Patina, scoffs at the idea, Leah disowns her with vitriolic fury. Bestowing instead the prize money upon her two eldest daughters, her dreams of a pampered retirement in the arms of her offspring for herself and her close companion, Pearl, seem guaranteed. Things soon turn sour, however, as long-held grievances and newfound wealth lead to familial treachery, violence and death.

Greed, lust, drugs, and Capodimonte combust in this low-rent, Southern fried twist on a literary classic.

The Meta Plays

A collection of short comedic plays that take theatrical conventions on a metaphysical joyride.

This unique compilation of wittily inventive short comedies can be performed by as few as 4 actors or as many as 18, all with minimal set and prop requirements. Many of these plays have gone on to receive highly successful productions around the world, garnering glowing reviews along the way.

Arcane Acts of Urban Renewal

Five One-Act Comedies Approx. 100 minutes

A collection of five thematically related, darkly humorous one-act plays in which ordinary people find themselves in the most extraordinary circumstances.

An Honest Mistake: Madge has long since surrendered herself to the verbal abuse doled out to her by her belligerent husband, Stan. On this particular evening, however, her fears of a rat beneath the floorboards, combined with her absent-mindedness, result in her dishing up Stan not only his evening meal - but also his just deserts!

A Familiar Face: Two elderly women, old friends, meet up in a London café shortly after one them – Dora – has been widowed. As Dora's grief and anger intensifies, her good friend Eydie begins to suspect there may be more to her angst than the loss of a loved one. When Dora calmly removes from her shopping bag a large glass jar containing a human head, discussions over its mysterious identity, and how it came to be lodged in the cupboard under her stairs, lead to some startling revelations.

A Slip of the Tongue: Miss Perkins, tired of the constant innuendos and sexual insinuations of her employer, Mr. Reams, has decided to hand in her notice. On this particular morning, however, Mr. Reams decides to take things one step further. Unfortunately, due to Miss Perkins' nervous disposition and a telephone that rings at a disturbingly high pitch, he soon discovers he's bitten off more than he can chew...or at least, one of them has.

An Embarrassing Odour: Ethel, a widowed pensioner, sits down one evening to tackle her daily crossword puzzle. Suddenly her tranquil world is turned upside down when a burglar enters her home, believing it to be unoccupied. As Ethel vainly attempts to forge a relationship with the violent delinquent before her, his concerns lie only with getting his hands on her valuables...that and the unpleasant smell that fills the room. What is that smell?

A Stunning Confession: During an evening in front of the television a staid married couple suddenly find themselves having to confront a new reality.

Suburban Redux

3M/1F or 2M/2F Approx. 90 minutes

After thirty years of arid matrimony and suburban monotony, Mrs. Pennington-South's only dream was that her son, Cuthbert, would break free of the cycle of upper-middle class inertia that had suffocated her. Raising him in the hope that he was homosexual, she soon begins dragging home potential suitors for tea – on this particular occasion a rather shy, awkward young man named Tristram. Cuthbert, however, finds he can no longer maintain his façade and at last confesses to his mother his guilty secret: his heterosexuality.

When Cuthbert leaves to meet Trixie, his new female friend, Mrs. Pennington-South – heartbroken but accepting – takes solace in the company of Tristram, and a mutual love of the arts soon leads to a new found friendship. After several weeks, however, Tristram's feelings take on more amorous overtones, and a confession of love for a woman almost thirty years his senior sends Mrs. Pennington-South into a state of emotional turmoil. Her anxiety is further heightened by the unexpected arrival of Cuthbert, merrily announcing that he has brought Trixie home for an introduction, and of the "big news" they wish to impart.

Mrs. Pennington-South, mortified at having to face the reality of her son's lifestyle choice, fearfully awaits the dreaded Trixie. Nothing, however, could have prepared her for what would come next.

A Ballyhoo in Blighty

The multi-award winning, critically acclaimed "Indigenous Peoples" (Winner "Best Play" – New York's Wonderland One-Act Festival) is paired with three other cheeky, uproarious comedies in what is guaranteed to be an unforgettable, side-splitting evening's entertainment.

Also included are "The Man Who Liked Dick", "Kitchen Sink Drama" and "Carbon-Based Life Form Seeks Similar" – all outrageously funny British comedies that have received lauded productions in London, New York and beyond.

Cast size: 4M / 5F (Roles can be doubled for a 2M/2F cast configuration)

Printed in Great Britain
by Amazon